THE WORLD OF ENERGY

Understanding
FOSSIL FUELS

POLLY GOODMAN

Gareth Stevens
Publishing

Please visit our Web site, www.garethstevens.com. For a free color catalog of all our high-quality books, call toll free 1-800-542-2595 or fax 1-877-542-2596.

Library of Congress Cataloging-in-Publication Data

Goodman, Polly.
 Understanding fossil fuels / Polly Goodman.
     p. cm. — (The world of energy)
 Includes index.
 ISBN 978-1-4339-4118-4 (library binding)
 1. Fossil fuels—Juvenile literature. I. Title.
 TP318.3.G65 2011
 665.5—dc22

                              2010015843

This edition first published in 2011 by
Gareth Stevens Publishing
111 East 14th Street, Suite 349
New York, NY 10003

Editorial Director: Kerri O'Donnell
Art Director: Haley Harasymiw

Photo Credits:
Canada House: pages 6, 20–21; Corbis 33 (Paul Buck/epa), 43 bottom (xinhua/Xinhua Press); e.t. archive: page 10; Ecoscene: pages 15 (Gryniewcz), 24 (Erik Schaffer), 30, 30–31 (Sally Morgan), 32 (Gryniewcz), 36–37 (Alan Towse), 38 (Sally Morgan); Mary Evans Photo Library: pages 8, 11, 12; Eye Ubiquitous: pages 13 (Steve Lindridge), 16–17 (David Cumming), 25 (Tim Hawkins), 28 (Davy Bold); Forlaget Flachs: pages 26–27 (Enequist Kommunikation), 35 (Olë Steen Hansen), 41 bottom and 43 bottom (Olë Steen Hansen), 41 top (D.O.N.G.); Hodder Wayland Photo Library: pages 18 (BP); National Coal Board: page 42; Nissan Motors: page 34; Samfoto: pages 9 (Ragnar Frislid), 16 (Svein Erik Dahl), 20 right (Svein Erik Dahl), 23 (Hans Hvide Bang); Science Photo Library: pages 4 bottom (Crown Copyright/Health and Safty Laboratory), 5 (Simon Fraser), 45 (Martin Bond); Shell Photo Service: page 29; Shutterstock.com *cover* and 1, 37 (Peter Baxter), 43 top (Aynia Brennan), 44 (Jose Gil); US Department of Energy: pages 4 top, 16, 20.

Printed in China
CPSIA compliance information: Batch #WAS10GS: For further information contact Gareth Stevens, New York, New York at 1-800-542-2595.

CONTENTS

WHAT ARE FOSSIL FUELS?

Fossil fuels are coal, oil, and natural gas. We use these fuels for energy, for heating and lighting, and to drive machines. They are burned to release their energy.

Every day, we use energy from fossil fuels. We burn coal, oil, and gas in our homes for heating and cooking. Most of the electricity we use is made by power plants that burn coal or oil.

Cars, buses, and other vehicles burn gasoline or diesel oil in their engines. We use them to travel from place to place.

▲ An oil-drilling tower at the Elk Hills oil field, in Alaska.

◄ A machine cuts coal inside an underground coal mine. The man in the front of the picture is measuring the noise level, to make sure it is safe for the other workers in the mine.

Steam pours from the cooling towers of the Ferrybridge power plant in Yorkshire, UK. ▼

How Were They Formed?

Coal, oil, and natural gas were formed over millions of years. They are made from the remains of plants and animals. Most coal began to form about 300 million years ago, when swamps covered much of the Earth. Tall plants grew in the swamps. When they died, they piled up together in layers. The layers became compressed (or squashed), one on top of the other.

As the layers became compressed, at first they formed peat. Then they formed lignite, or brown coal. Finally, they formed anthracite, or black coal.

Oil and gas formed under the seas, from the remains of microscopic plants and animals. Under the sea, the compressed layers formed liquid oil, instead of coal. They also gave off gas. The oil and gas was trapped in pockets between the rocks around them. Now these areas are oil and gas fields.

◄ *A machine digs up tar sands in Alberta, Canada. Tar sands contain oil and gas, which can be extracted (or taken out) by mixing the sands with steam and water.*

AN OIL AND GAS PLATFORM
A drill cuts down through layers of rock to reach pockets of oil and gas underground. ▼

Platform

FORMATION OF COAL
1. Tall ferns and other plants grow in swamps.
2. Plants die and are covered by other plants and mud.
3. Layers of dead plants are compressed underground. ▼

Rock layers

Trapped gas

Oil

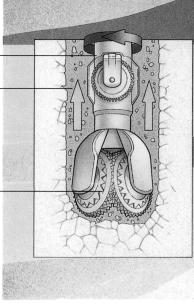

1

2

3

THE DRILL

Spinning drill

Mud is pumped down the well and then carries rock to the surface

Teeth break up the rock

Coal

Coal has been used for thousands of years. The first people to use it were probably the Chinese, about 3,000 years ago. Later, it was used by other ancient civilizations, including the Greeks and Romans in Europe, and the Hopi Indians in North America.

A drawing of a coal mine in 1885. There were no machines, so the miners used hand picks, shovels, and horse-drawn carts to collect the coal. ▼

Steam engines were invented in the 1700s. They burned huge amounts of coal to make steam power. Steam engines ran machines in factories, so they helped the growth of industries in the 1800s. ▶

Mining

At first, coal was dug from hillsides and open pits using hand tools. By 300 CE, the Chinese were mining coal near the surface of the ground. In Europe, coal mining started in the 1200s, but it was not until the 1600s that the industry really took off in the UK.

Until the 1600s, all coal mining was done by hand. In the 1600s, ponies were taken down coal mines and used to pull carts full of coal. They were known as pit ponies. In the 1800s, steam engines were used to pump out water and pull up coal from the mines.

Oil

Like coal, oil has been used for thousands of years. The ancient Egyptians covered the bodies of their dead, called mummies, in thick oil hardened by the sunlight. Other ancient civilizations, such as the Chinese and the Native Americans, used oil for heat, light, and medicine.

The Chinese first drilled oil in the second century BCE. They used bamboo pipes and bronze tubes. But until the nineteenth century, most oil was found in pools on the surface, or discovered by accident when digging wells.

The modern oil industry began in 1859 in the U.S.A. Steam was used to power the drills.

The ribs and legs of an ancient Egyptian mummy, which has been covered in oil. ▶

In 1859, Edwin L. Drake first used steam power to drill for oil in Pennsylvania. A few years later, drilling towers covered the hills of Pennsylvania. ▶

Gas

The ancient Chinese were the first people to use natural gas. They found it when they dug wells to look for salt water. They burned the gas to boil off the water and leave the salt behind.

In 1739, a British clergyman named John Clayton found out how to make gas from coal. In 1792, a British inventor first lit his home using coal gas. Soon after, many streets in the UK had lamps. The light was made from coal gas.

● Coal
● Oil
● Natural gas

▲ *A lamplighter lights a gas street lamp in London, UK, in 1867.*

This map shows the places where coal, oil, and natural gas are found around the world. Some recent discoveries are gas fields in the North Sea, Russia, Canada, Australia, and the Gulf of Mexico. ▶

▲ *A modern gas platform. The flame lets out bursts of gas.*

Natural Gas

The natural gas industry first started in the United States, in the middle of the nineteenth century. There were no long-distance pipelines to carry the gas far, so people had to live close to the gas fields.

After 1930, steel pipelines were made, which could carry gas across long distances.

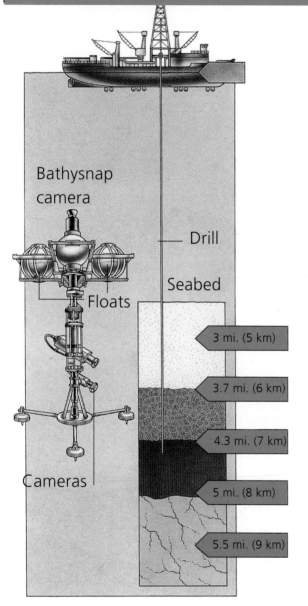

Bathysnap
camera

Drill

Seabed

Floats

3 mi. (5 km)

3.7 mi. (6 km)

4.3 mi. (7 km)

5 mi. (8 km)

5.5 mi. (9 km)

Cameras

▲ *This diagram shows a ship doing a test drill for oil. The Bathysnap camera is dropped onto the seabed. After it has taken pictures, it floats to the surface.*

Before any drilling or mining begins, experts have to find, or prospect for, stores of fossil fuels underground. In the past, this search relied on a lot of luck. Many wells were dug without success.

Today, scientists make a map of what is under the ground. This is called surveying. They look for certain types of rock that are likely to contain fossil fuels.

Some clues, such as the magnetic field and gravity of an area, give details about the type and density of rock underground. Explosions are used to measure how sound waves travel through rock. Samples of rock are drilled and studied.

FACT FILE

Over 100 years ago, oil men who explored the "Wild West" area of the United States often came across wild big cats, which they killed and hung on the drilling towers. Wells drilled in new places often became known as "wildcats."

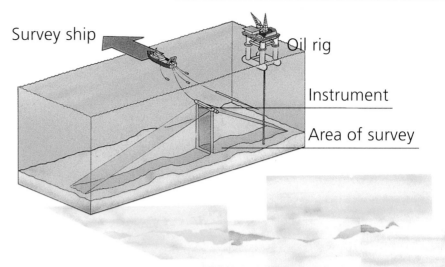

Survey ship

Oil rig

Instrument

Area of survey

▲ *Survey ships take pictures of the seabed. They use a special instrument, which is dragged behind the ship.*

◄ *Layers of sandstone and mudstone in Wales. These rocks are sedimentary rocks, like coal, but they formed earlier than coal.*

Miners wear protective helmets with electric lamps. ▼

This huge drill is used to extract coal. As the drill turns, the teeth around its edge bite into the coal. ▼

Coal Mining

Modern coal mining is done by machines, but people are still needed to operate them. The machines cut the coal, hold up the roof, and carry coal and miners up and down the mine shaft.

If the coal is near the surface, it is mined from open pits. These are called open-pit mines. If the coal is over 200 feet (60 m) below the ground, mines are dug deep underground.

At an open-pit mine in Germany, coal is crushed, washed, and poured into piles. ▶

When mines are dug underground, first a shaft is dug down to reach the coal. Miners dig outward from the shaft.

After the coal has been cut, it is brought to the surface. Then it is blasted with explosives to separate it from the rock and crushed. Finally, it is scooped up by huge shovels and washed.

FACT FILE

There are two main methods of underground mining. In longwall mining, the roof falls in behind the cutting machine. In room-and-pillar mining, the cutting machine leaves pillars of coal to hold up the roof.

17

Gas is carried to this terminal in Yorkshire, UK, in pipelines from the North Sea. ▼

Drilling for Oil and Gas

To reach oil and gas underground, a sharp, spinning drill cuts through the earth (see page 7). The drill is joined to a pipe. As the drill sinks under the ground, more pipe is added to the top. The pipe can be several miles long by the time the drill reaches oil or gas.

To help the drill cut through rock, liquid mud is pumped down the pipe. The mud washes away pieces of rock and helps drive the drill.

When the drill finally reaches the oil, it can let out a huge amount of pressure. The oil can burst out of the top of the pipe in a "blowout" or "gusher." Special valves at the top of the pipe stop blowouts.

Water and gas can help force oil out of a well. A "nodding donkey" machine forces steam into an oil well. The steam helps to push the oil up and out of the shaft. ▶

Drill ships can take oil from the deepest waters, as deep as 7,845 feet (2,400 m). They stay in exactly the same place using a global positioning system (GPS) and special propellers. ▼

Offshore Oil Rigs

Oil under the seabed is drilled by offshore oil rigs. They can be as big as skyscrapers. In shallow seas, rigs stand on the seabed as far down as 1,312 feet (400 m) below the surface of the wate In deep water, rigs float on the surface, anchorec to the seabed up to 3,280 feet (1,000 m) below.

This is an offshore oil rig near the coast of Norway. Workers live at the top. ▶

This island was made specially for an oil rig. It is in the shallow Beaufort Sea, near the coast of Canada. ▼

FACT FILE

The world's main offshore oil fields are under the Arabian Gulf, the Gulf of Mexico, and the North Sea.

There are large amounts of oil and gas under the North Sea. The first gas field was discovered in 1959. Then oil was discovered in 1969.

The North Sea is a difficult place to drill for oil. Offshore oil rigs stand in water as deep as 590 feet (180 m). Waves can be 100 feet (30 m) high and winds blow at 75 miles (120 km) an hour.

The gas and oil is brought to the shore on oil tankers and along pipelines over 620 miles (1,000 km) long.

Oil is brought to the surface through pipelines. It is held in storage tanks until oil tankers take it away from a filling tower. ▼

Oil tanker

Filling tower

Oil rig

Storage tanks

New Oil Fields

The Buzzard oil field was discovered in 2001. It lies 60 miles (100 km) northeast of Aberdeen, Scotland, and is thought to have a total of 550 million barrels of oil.

Oil companies are looking for new oil fields to the west of Scotland, too, where conditions are much harder. Oil rigs will have to float on the surface because the seas are so deep.

FACT FILE

A huge oil field was found in the Gulf of Mexico in 2009, about 250 miles (400 km) southwest of Houston, Texas.

The Ekofisk oil field in the North Sea was found at the end of 1969. ▼

Refining Oil

After oil is drilled from underground, it goes to an oil refinery. Oil that comes out of the ground is called crude oil. It is only useful if it is separated into different parts. This is done in an oil refinery.

Crude oil is separated into gases, gasoline, kerosene, diesel, engine oil, fuel oil, waxes, and tar.

▲ *An oil refinery in Puerto Rico.*

Pipelines in an oil refinery. ▼

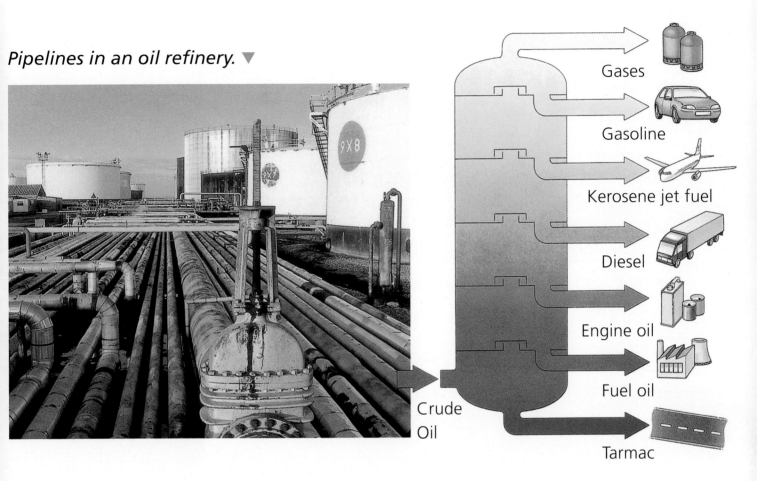

Gases

Gasoline

Kerosene jet fuel

Diesel

Engine oil

Fuel oil

Tarmac

Crude Oil

Distillation

Heat, pressure, and chemicals are used to distill crude oil. This separates it into different parts. At first, the oil is heated in a distillation tower.

Heat makes the lightest oils and gases rise to the top. The heavier oils stay at the bottom.

The crude oil is separated into chemicals. These can be made into plastics, detergents, fibers, medicines, and other materials.

▲ *A distillation tower separates crude oil into different materials. You can see the everyday products each material is used for.*

An Oil Refinery

When oil first arrives at a refinery, it is pumped into tanks. Then it is piped into distillation towers, where it is distilled.

Next, the separated materials are piped to other parts of the refinery. They are treated to separate them even more. For example, heavy oils are cooled to remove the waxes in them. A process called "cracking" helps to get more gasoline from heavy oil.

Finally, all the different products are put in storage tanks, ready to be sold and taken to where they will be used.

◄ *This diagram shows some of the everyday products made from crude oil.*

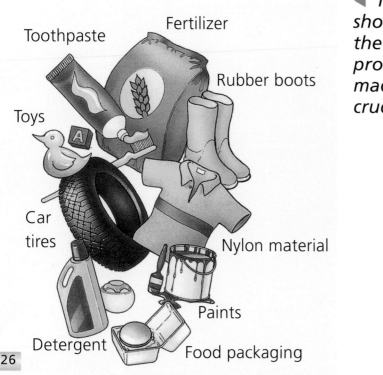

Toothpaste
Fertilizer
Rubber boots
Toys
Car tires
Nylon material
Paints
Detergent
Food packaging

FACT FILE

The biggest oil refinery in the world is in Texas. It can store more than 572,000 barrels of oil.

The Frederica oil refinery in Denmark. Like all refineries, this one works 24 hours a day. ▼

▲ *A tanker truck carries products away from an oil refinery.*

Moving Oil

Oil is carried around the world in supertankers. Each of these huge ships can carry 450,000 tons (400,000 tonnes) of oil. On land, oil is carried in enormous pipelines. In cold countries, the pipes have to be kept warm, to stop the oil from getting too thick.

Moving Gas

Gas from gas fields close to land is carried ashore by pipeline. But over longer distances, gas is carried by supertankers. To make it take up less space, gas is made into a liquid by cooling it to under 322.7° F (161.5° C).

Moving Products

Products from oil refineries are carried by road using tanker trucks, or by train using tanker wagons.

Supertankers are too big to enter many oil terminals. So they unload oil into smaller tankers. ▶

Supertankers carry crude oil in separate compartments, to stop the weight of the oil rolling the ship over. ▼

Control rooms

Separate oil compartments

◄ *Power stations in the former East Germany burned a poor grade of coal, called brown coal, or lignite. It caused serious air pollution over Europe.*

Fossil Fuels and the Environment

When fossil fuels are burned, they release gases into the air. The gases cause air pollution and acid rain. Many scientists believe that they also heat up the Earth's atmosphere, making the climate warmer. This is called global warming.

Smog is a mixture of smoke and fog that pollutes the air. In many cities today, it happens when chemicals from gasoline engines mix with air. This is called photochemical smog. The weather can trap the smog over a city, making it difficult for people to breathe.

Acid rain is caused when gases from burning fossil fuels mix with water in clouds. When it rains, the water from the clouds has acid in it. The acid kills plants, damages buildings, and pollutes rivers.

◄ *A blue smog hangs over Hong Kong Island.*

FACT FILE

In the past, most smog was caused by burning coal for heat. Today, photochemical smog is caused by car fumes.

On February 15, 1996, an oil tanker called the *Sea Empress* ran aground near the coast of Wales, spilling 6,720 tons (6,000 tonnes) of oil into the sea.

Tugboats tried to hold the tanker in place using cables. But strong gales snapped the cables and the tanker ran aground again.

Finally, six days later, the tanker was secured. By that time, over 81,760 tons (73,000 tonnes) of oil had spilled into the sea.

Cleaning up the oil spill was a huge task. In the sea, oil floats on water. So floating barriers, called booms, helped stop the oil from spreading. It was skimmed off the surface and collected in tanks.

On land, it was a more difficult task. The oil was scraped off beaches and blasted off rocks using jets of water.

Workers struggle to clear crude oil from Welsh beaches, after the oil tanker Sea Empress *ran aground in February 1996.* ▶

FACT FILE

The world's worst spill from an oil tanker was in 1979.

Two supertankers collided in the Caribbean Sea and spilled 313,600 tons (280,000 tonnes) of oil.

Oil and Wildlife

Oil spills kill thousands of seabirds, seals, and fish. Most wildlife is poisoned by oil, and often by the chemicals used to clean up the spill.

A huge oil spill in the Gulf of Mexico happened in 2010 when an oil well blew out and caused an oil rig to explode. Thousands of barrels of oil a day leaked into the sea. The oil quickly spread, killing an untold number of fish, birds, and sea mammals.

▲ *A fisherman watches as oil spreads in the Gulf of Mexico, in 2010.*

33

USING FOSSIL FUELS

Fossil fuels are used for energy. When they are burned, they release their energy in the form of heat.

In engines, heat from fossil fuels makes gases expand quickly. The force of this is used to make the engine work.

In the gasoline engine of a car, a spark lights up gasoline inside a cylinder. The heat expands the gases in the air. The force pushes a piston, which helps drive the wheels of the car.

◄ *A computer in this modern gasoline engine makes sure that no fuel is wasted.*

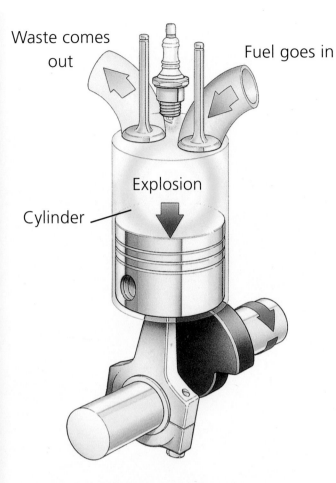

Waste comes out

Fuel goes in

Explosion

Cylinder

▲ When fuel enters the gasoline engine of a car, it is lit by a spark, which makes a small explosion. The explosion drives the car wheels.

Diesel engines do not use a spark to light the fuel. They squeeze the fuel so much that it heats up and burns.

Jet engines burn fossil fuels. But instead of making a series of explosions like a gasoline engine, they burn fuels continuously.

Diesel-electric engines are divided into two parts. A diesel engine makes electricity. The electricity makes the power.

This airplane has four jet engines, leaving trails of black smoke behind. ▼

Hot-air balloons burn propane gas to make the air inside them lighter than the air around. This helps them rise up in the air. ▶

Every Day

We use fossil fuels every day. Gas is used for cooking and heating in our homes, schools, and offices. Gasoline and diesel help us get around. Most of our electricity is made in power plants that burn oil or coal.

Gas is very useful because it can be compressed into a small space. This makes it easy to carry around. Campers and mountaineers carry bottled gas with them to help them cook anywhere. Hot-air balloons use bottled gas to heat up the air and help them rise.

FACT FILE

Bunsen burners are gas burners. Their flame can be made bigger by letting more air mix with the gas.

▲ Many barbecue grills use piped gas, such as butane.

▲ *Steam rises out of the cooling towers of Ferrybridge power plant, in Yorkshire, UK. This is a coal and biomass-fired power plant.*

Power Plants

Not all power plants burn fossil fuels. Some use nuclear, wind, or water power. Most power plants burn coal or oil, but some burn biomass (a fuel made from plants and animals), too.

In coal-fired power plants, heat from burning coal turns water into steam. The steam drives the generators that make electricity. Coal and oil-fired power plants burn hundreds of tons of coal and oil every day. So coal-fired power plants are usually built near coal fields, and oil-fired power plants are usually built near oil refineries.

Waste

Power plants that burn fossil fuels waste a lot of energy. More heat is made from burning fuels than is used to heat the water. Most of this heat is not used.

Some power plants in the Scandinavian countries use the extra heat. Special pipes under the power plants carry the heat to homes and offices.

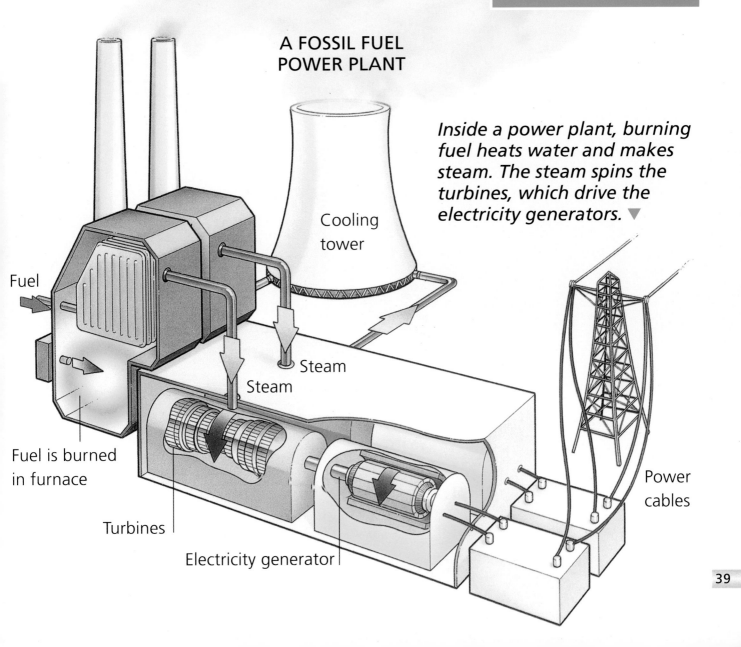

A FOSSIL FUEL POWER PLANT

Inside a power plant, burning fuel heats water and makes steam. The steam spins the turbines, which drive the electricity generators. ▼

Cooling tower

Fuel

Steam

Steam

Fuel is burned in furnace

Turbines

Electricity generator

Power cables

Before the 1980s, Denmark's main fuels were oil and coal. Oil was expensive because it was imported from the Middle East.

In 1959, natural gas fields were discovered in the North Sea. If the country could use gas instead of oil, it would be much cheaper. So in 1979, Denmark started to build pipelines to carry gas from the North Sea.

Gas is a cleaner fuel to burn than coal or oil. By burning gas instead of oil, Denmark has lowered its levels of air pollution.

FACT FILE

Over half of all Danish homes are now heated by gas piped from the North Sea.

This map shows Denmark's gas and oil pipelines. ▼

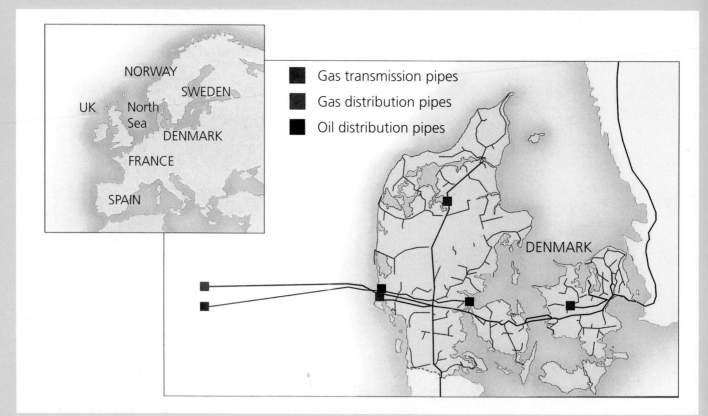

NORWAY

SWEDEN

UK   North Sea

DENMARK

FRANCE

SPAIN

■ Gas transmission pipes

■ Gas distribution pipes

■ Oil distribution pipes

DENMARK

Coal

Coal is still one of Denmark's main fuels. Most of it is burned in power plants to make electricity.

When it is burned, coal makes more carbon dioxide than any other fossil fuel. This causes air pollution and may help to warm the Earth's climate. So Denmark is trying to use wind power instead of coal, to make electricity.

◀ *Gas pipelines being laid in Denmark. The pipelines have to run under many small seas in this country.*

◀ *This power plant burns coal to make electricity. It also makes heat, which is carried away in hot water and used to heat people's homes.*

Burning fossil fuels pollutes the Earth's environment. Today, many people are worried that emissions (poisonous gases) from burning fossil fuels might also be the cause of global warming, or climate change. This may cause the sea levels to rise and coastlands and islands will become flooded.

Fossil fuels are also running out or becoming harder to extract from the Earth. We need to find different kinds of power to use.

Climate Change Meeting

In 2009, world leaders met at the United Nations Climate Change Conference in Copenhagen, Denmark. They talked about what governments can do to stop the climate from warming up more than 3.6° F (2° C). President Obama and other leaders set up the Copenhagen Accord (an agreement), which says that countries should do all they can to reduce emissions in the air.

Governments can help by developing alternative kinds of energy, such as wind power, water power, and solar power, which do not cause as much pollution. They can also help by making public transportation better and cheaper.

▲ Coal that is made into a liquid has less sulfur than solid coal. This means it is a cleaner fuel to burn. It causes less air pollution.

◀ People protest against governments that do not want to do enough to stop climate change at the Copenhagen conference.

FACT FILE

There is much more coal left in the world than oil or gas. So once oil and gas run out, coal may be used even more. We must find cleaner ways of using it.

◀ President Obama and other world leaders took part in the Copenhagen Climate Change Conference in Denmark in 2009. They discussed new ways to reduce fossil fuel emissions.

New Fuels

Hydrogen is a gas that can be used as a fuel. When it burns, it makes water vapor instead of harmful gases, so it is much cleaner than coal or oil.

Hydrogen can be made from fossil fuels. But it can also be made from water. This means that when fossil fuels run out, it will still be possible to make hydrogen fuel.

Scientists are trying to find more efficient ways of using hydrogen instead of fossil fuels. One way is to use it in fuel cells.

FACT FILE

In the late 1960s and 1970s, the U.S. Apollo space program sent spacecraft to explore the moon. The spacecraft used fuel cells to make electricity and drinking water for the astronauts.

This car uses hydrogen instead of gasoline. ▼

A diagram of a fuel cell. ▼

Electricity

Hydrogen (H$_2$)

Oxygen (O$_2$)

Water (H$_2$O)

▲ *This engineer is putting fuel cells together.*

Fuel Cells and Electric Cars

A fuel cell mixes hydrogen and oxygen to make electricity. The only waste product is water. So fuel cells are a very clean source of power.

Fuel cells are expensive, but they are getting cheaper as technology improves. They may be used more and more in electric vehicles in the future.

Water (H$_2$O)

Hydrogen (H$_2$)

Oxygen (O$_2$)

Hydrogen (H$_2$)

▲ *Water can be split into hydrogen and oxygen. The chemical symbol for each substance is in parentheses.*

GLOSSARY

Acid rain Rain that contains pollution from factories and traffic.

Atmosphere The gases that surround Earth.

Biomass Organic material made from plants and animals.

Booms Floating barriers, used to stop oil spills from spreading in the sea.

Butane A colorless gas made from crude oil in a refinery.

Compressed Squashed.

Crude oil Pure oil that has just come from underground.

Cylinder An object shaped like a roller or tube, which can be hollow or solid.

Density The thickness or compactness of something.

Distill Purify by heating up and then cooling down.

Emissions Gases given out by something, such as burning fossil fuels.

Environment Everything in our natural surroundings: the earth, air, and water.

Expand To grow larger.

Extracted Taken out.

Generators Machines that make electricity.

Global warming The rise in temperature of Earth's atmosphere. Also known as climate change.

Grades Different qualities of something.

Gravity The natural force that attracts objects toward the center of Earth.

Imported Brought in from a foreign country.

Magnetic field The area around a magnet where its power of attraction works.

Microscopic Objects that cannot be seen without using a microscope.

Mummies Dead bodies that have been specially treated to keep them from decaying.

Piston Two cylinders, one inside the other, that go up and down. Pistons are used to make engines or pumps work.

Pollute To make dirty.

Propane gas A colorless gas made from oil or natural gas.

Prospecting Exploring an area to look for oil, gold, or other minerals.

Refinery A building used to distill crude oil. There are also sugar and metal refineries, used to purify sugar and metal.

Sedimentary rocks Rocks formed from material tha has been deposited by water, wind, or ice.

Surveying Examining an area.

Tar sand Sand covered with a substance that produces oil.

Terminal Either end of a route where goods are loaded or unloaded.

Turbines Engines or moto that are made to work by the power of water, steam or air.

Waste The substances left over after something has been used.

FURTHER INFORMATION

Further Reading

The Energy Debate: The Pros and Cons of Coal, Gas, and Oil
by Sally Morgan
Rosen Central, 2007

Energy Today: Coal, Oil, and Natural Gas
by Geoffrey M. Horn
Chelsea House Publications, 2010

Powering the Future: New Energy Technologies
by Eva Thaddeus
University of New Mexico Press, 2010

Web Sites

http://home.clara.net/darvill/altenerg/fossil.htm

http://science.howstuffworks.com/gasoline.htm

http://www.teachcoal.org/aboutcoal/articles/coalconvert.html

ENERGY CONSUMPTION
The use of energy is measured in joules per second, or watts. Different machines use up different amounts of energy. The diagram on the right gives a few examples. ▶

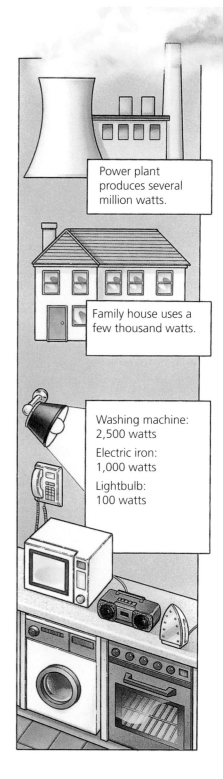

Power plant produces several million watts.

Family house uses a few thousand watts.

Washing machine: 2,500 watts

Electric iron: 1,000 watts

Lightbulb: 100 watts

INDEX